Usborne ART ideas
How to Knit

Fiona Watt

Designed by Erica Harrison

Illustrated by Stella Baggott
Photographs by Howard Allman

Contents

Materials

These pages show you some of the things you will need before you start to learn how to knit. You can find them in many craft stores, specialist wool shops or on the Internet.

Knitting needles

Knitting needles come in a variety of sizes. The thicker the needle, the bigger the stitches will be. Knitting patterns will tell you the size of needle to use. Find out more about the size of needles on pages 7 and 63.

Long pins with large heads

A sharp pair of scissors

Throughout the book all the knitting is actual size unless it says otherwise.

The pink yarn above is called medium weight.

This bulky yarn was used to make the felted bag on page 47.

This purse was knitted using light weight yarn.

Yarn

There are lots of different types of yarn made from different kinds of materials. They also vary in thickness and this is known as its 'weight'. Most beginners find it easiest to learn using a medium weight yarn. See pages 6-7 for more about different types of yarn.

Sewing needle

Stitch holder

A stitch holder is like a large safety pin and is used to hold spare stitches while you shape your knitting. They are used for the ribbed scarf on pages 28-29 and the heart cushion on pages 44-45.

Tape measure

You will also need a tape measure to measure the length of your knitting. If you don't have a tape measure, use a long ruler instead.

Sewing needle

You will need a blunt sewing needle with a large eye so that the yarn will go through. This is used for sewing in loose ends of yarn left when you join on a new ball, and for sewing the edges of your knitting together.

Pins

If you are knitting something that will be sewn together, such as a bag or a purse, you will need some pins to secure the edges as you sew. Long pins with large plastic heads are the best to use.

Tape measure

Stitch holder

Buttons

Decorations

Some of the knitting in this book is decorated with beads, buttons and sequins. Look on page 38 to find out how to sew buttons onto the things you have knitted. Other items have had patterns sewn onto them with embroidery thread. Find out on pages 58-59 how to do different stitches.

Complete beginners often find fluffy yarns like this difficult to knit with. Start with a 'smooth' yarn instead.

Beads and sequins

Embroidery thread

5

Thick and thin yarns

At the beginning of each project you will find the type of yarn you will need, and the size of needle to knit with. If you use a different thickness of yarn or different needles from the ones suggested, then your knitting won't turn out to be the same size as the examples in the book.

Weight of yarn

There are lots of different kinds of yarn, and they are described by their 'weight,' such as medium or bulky. Unfortunately this isn't often shown on the paper band wrapped around a ball of yarn. Ask an assistant in the shop to help you find the correct weight of yarn for your knitting.

All these samples of knitting were knitted on size 5mm (US 8) needles, but with different weights of yarn.

The pale yellow sample was knitted with a fine weight.

This cream yarn is double knitting weight.

The green yarn is medium weight.

Compare the sizes of these three samples. The thicker the yarn, the bigger your knitting will be.

Gauge or tension

Most knitting patterns mention something called the 'gauge' or 'tension' of yarn. This is the number of stitches and the number of rows that you get when you measure a 10cm (4 inch) square on your knitting.

Knitting the correct gauge is important when you are making clothes, so that they fit properly. It's not something you need to worry about with the patterns in this book though, just use the yarn and the needles suggested.

Dye lots

Yarn is usually dyed in batches and one batch may not be exactly the same shade as another. Each batch is given something called a 'dye lot number' which you'll find on the yarn's paper band. So, if you need more than one ball of yarn make sure that the numbers match when you buy your yarn.

Knitting needles are usually made from metal, plastic or wood.

These needles are shown actual size. The thinnest of these knitting needles is 4mm (US 4) and the largest is 12mm (US 17).

Needle size

The knitting needle sizes in this book are shown in millimeters (mm), but there are two other measurements used in knitting patterns. They are called Old UK and US (see page 63 for a conversion chart).

Information on a ball band

All paper bands on balls of yarn are different, but most of them show the same kind of information, such as the weight of the yarn, a color or shade number and the yarn's dye lot. It also shows the size of needle which is best to use with the yarn.

Tension or gauge of the yarn

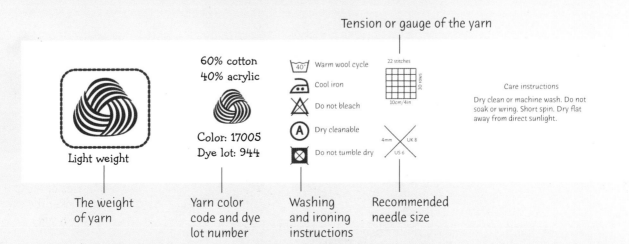

60% cotton
40% acrylic

Color: 17005
Dye lot: 944

Light weight

- Warm wool cycle
- Cool iron
- Do not bleach
- Dry cleanable
- Do not tumble dry

22 stitches
30 rows
10cm/4in

Care instructions
Dry clean or machine wash. Do not soak or wring. Short spin. Dry flat away from direct sunlight.

4mm — UK 8
US 6

The weight of yarn

Yarn color code and dye lot number

Washing and ironing instructions

Recommended needle size

Starting out

Before you start to knit, you will need to make stitches on one of your knitting needles. This is called casting on. Knitters cast on in lots of different ways. One of the easiest ways is called the 'thumb method' or 'long tail cast-on' which is shown on the page opposite.

The first thing you need to do is make a slip knot – this will be your first stitch.

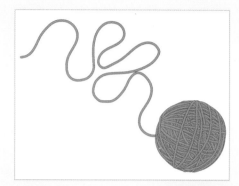

1. Start by unwinding about 20 inches from a ball of yarn – this is roughly the length of your arm.

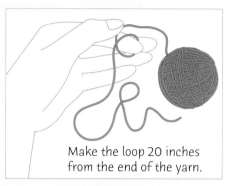

Make the loop 20 inches from the end of the yarn.

2. Make a loose loop in the yarn by wrapping it around your first finger. Hold the loop with your thumb.

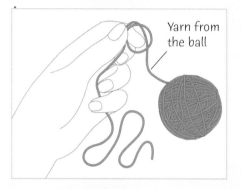

Yarn from the ball

3. Let the yarn from the ball (not the loose long tail) fall behind the loop on your finger, like this.

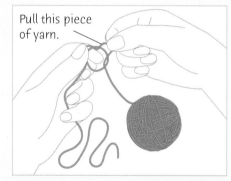

Pull this piece of yarn.

4. Take hold of the yarn between the first finger and thumb of your right hand, and pull it through the loop.

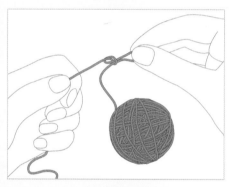

5. Let go of the loop in your left hand and pull the loose end gently downward to make a loose knot.

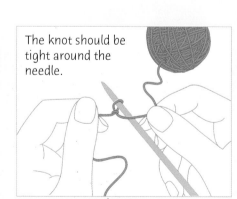

The knot should be tight around the needle.

6. Slide a knitting needle through the loop, then pull the yarn with the ball to tighten the knot.

It's not easy to predict how much yarn you should leave before you make the slip knot. Each pattern in this book tells you how much to unwind.

Casting on

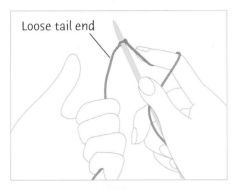

1. Hold the needle with the stitch in your right hand. Then, clasp the loose tail of the yarn under the fingers of your left hand, like this.

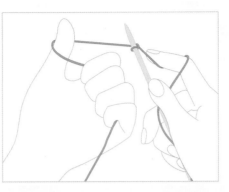

2. Wrap the yarn around the thumb on your left hand, then behind it by moving the needle and yarn in a circle above your thumb.

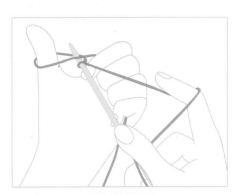

3. Slip the point of the needle under the yarn on your thumb. Wrap the yarn from the ball around the first finger on your right hand.

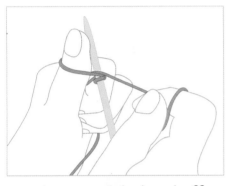

4. Take your right hand off the needle and wrap the yarn behind the needle, then bring it toward you between your thumb and the needle.

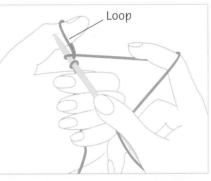

5. Hold the needle again. Slide your left thumb up to the tip of needle. Then, let the loop fall off your thumb and onto the needle.

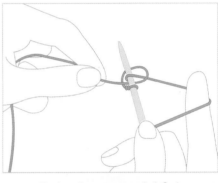

6. Pull the loose end of the yarn to tighten the stitch around the needle. Then, follow steps 1-5 again and again to add more stitches.

Try to keep your cast-on stitches as even as you can.

Starting to knit

Knit stitch

There are two main stitches used in knitting - knit and purl. This page shows you how to do knit stitch. There are different ways of doing this stitch. Look on page 60 for another method, which you may find easier, especially if you are left-handed.

Before you start, follow the instructions on pages 8-9 for casting on.

Wrap the yarn around your first finger.

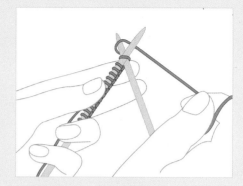

1. Hold the needle with the stitches in your left hand. Push the point of the other needle up into the first stitch from the front to the back.

2. Lift your hand off the right-hand needle and wrap the yarn around the back of the needle, then between the tips of the two needles.

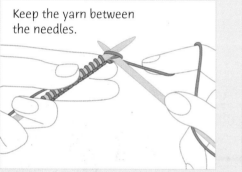
Keep the yarn between the needles.

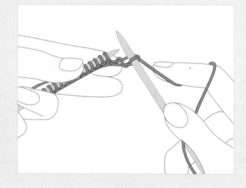

3. Take hold of the needle again in your right hand. Then, gradually slide the left-hand needle along the right-hand one, toward the tip.

4. Slide the left-hand needle over the tip of the right-hand one and down the back of it a little way. You'll now see a stitch on the right-hand needle.

5. Slide the right-hand needle along to the tip of the left-hand one, until the stitch slips off the tip. You've now knitted one stitch.

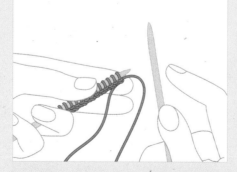

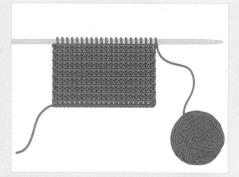

6. Pull the yarn in your right hand a little so that it tightens the stitch. Then, knit each stitch in the row in the same way.

7. When you've knitted every stitch in the first row, swap the needles over so that the one with the stitches is back in your left hand.

8. Continue knitting the stitches in each row in the same way. As you knit more rows your knitting will get longer and longer.

Picking up a dropped a stitch

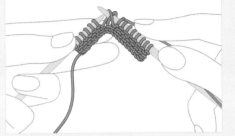

Push your needle in from the back to the front of the stitch.

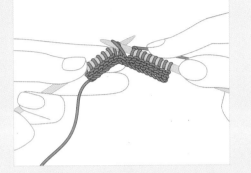

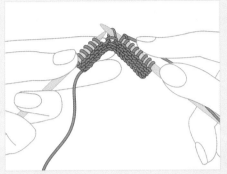

1. If you drop a stitch, push your right-hand needle into the stitch in the row below, and through the loop left from the dropped stitch.

2. Slip the tip of the left-hand needle through the stitch only from the front to the back. Don't push it through the loop.

3. Bring the left-hand needle over the tip of the right-hand one so the loop goes through the stitch. Pull the left-hand needle out of the stitch.

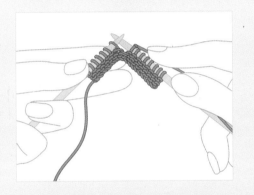

4. Transfer the stitch back onto the left-hand needle by slipping the tip of it into the stitch and pulling the right-hand needle out.

Casting off

When you have finished your knitting you need to secure all the stitches so that it doesn't unravel. This is called casting off.

If you want to knit a little scarf, like those shown here, cast on 7 stitches with light weight yarn on size 4.5mm (US 7) needles. Knit lots of rows until your knitting measures 18 inches. Then, cast off following these instructions.

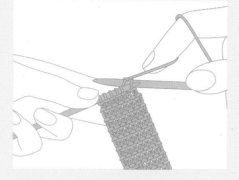

1. Knit two stitches, then push the tip of the left-hand needle into the front of the first stitch you have knitted, like this.

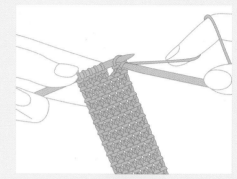

2. Slide the stitches to the tip of the right-hand needle. Then, lift the first stitch over the second one, keeping the yarn from the ball tight.

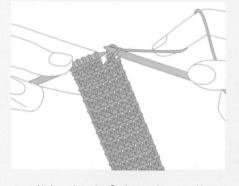

3. Slide the left-hand needle out of the stitch, so that there is only one stitch on the right-hand needle. Then, knit one more stitch.

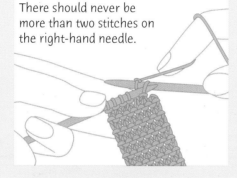

There should never be more than two stitches on the right-hand needle.

4. Push the left-hand needle into the first stitch on the right-hand needle again and lift it over the second stitch as you did in step 2.

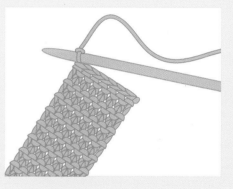

5. Continue casting off all the stitches in the row one by one in the same way, until you have one stitch left on the right-hand needle.

See page 14 for how to stitch in the loose ends.

6. Cut the yarn. Then, pull the needle to make the final stitch into a big loop. Then, push the yarn through the loop and pull it tight.

Find out on pages 36-37 how to add fringe like this to the end of the scarf.

Ironing your knitting

1. When you have finished your knitting it's a good idea to iron it. Lay it on an ironing board, then lay a clean kitchen towel on top.

Before you iron your knitting, check on the ball band to see if there are any special instructions.

2. Turn the iron on to a steam setting, then carefully iron over the knitting. Let any water on the towel cool before lifting it off.

If you want to knit a striped scarf, the steps on page 14 show you how to join on a new ball of yarn.

Making a scarf

You can make a simple scarf using knit stitch. This scarf uses two balls of yarn, so this page shows you how to join on a new ball of yarn.

You will need:
2 x 1¾ ounce balls of light or medium weight yarn
a pair of 4mm (US 6) or 4.5mm (US 7) knitting needles

Unwind about 20 inches of yarn, then make a slip knot.
Cast on 24 stitches.
First row - knit (K) to the end of the row.
Following rows - K until you use all the yarn on the first ball. (Don't knit right to the end of the yarn, leave at least 8 inches at the end of the last row).
Next row - join on the new ball of yarn following the instructions below, then K to the end of the row.
Continue knitting until you finish the second ball of yarn (or until the scarf is the length you want it to be).
Cast off.
Then, stitch in the loose ends of yarn (see below).

Joining a new ball of yarn

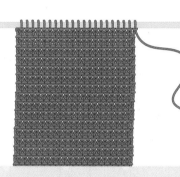

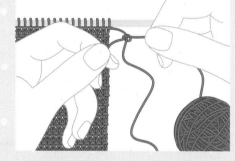

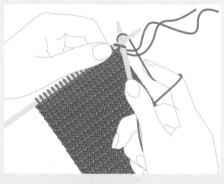

1. It's always best to join on a new ball of yarn at the end of a row, so finish a row, leaving at least 8 inches of yarn from the old ball.

2. Tie the new yarn around the old one with a loose knot. Then, slide the knot up to your knitting and pull it a little bit tighter.

3. As you do the first stitch in the row, wind the new yarn around the needle. You'll need to sew in the loose ends when you finish knitting.

Stitching in loose ends

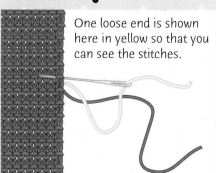

One loose end is shown here in yellow so that you can see the stitches.

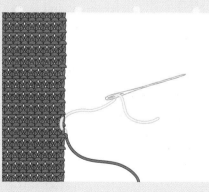

1. Thread the loose end of the yarn onto a needle with a large eye. Push the needle through the first stitch in the row above, like this.

2. Pull the yarn through the stitch, like this. Then, push your needle through a stitch in the row above and pull the yarn through again.

3. Continue weaving the yarn in and out of the stitches, for about eight stitches. Then, cut the yarn a little way away from your knitting.

If you want to add fringe
in the same color as your
scarf, don't knit all of the
second ball of yarn.

Purl stitch and stocking stitch
Purl stitch (P)

Most knitting uses a combination of purl stitch and knit stitch (see page 10). The type of knitting that you get when you do alternate rows of knit and purl stitches is called stocking stitch. It is smooth on one side and bumpy on the other.

Look on page 61 for instructions on how to purl using the 'Continental' way of knitting.

1. To make a square like those on the opposite page, cast on 21 stitches. Then, hold the needle with the stitches in your left hand.

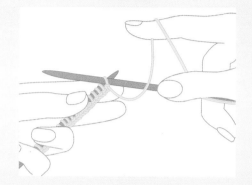

2. Push the right-hand needle into the first stitch so that it crosses over the left-hand needle. Then, bring the yarn in front of the needles.

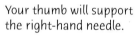
Your thumb will support the right-hand needle.

3. Hold the tip of the right-hand needle under your thumb. Then, wrap the yarn around the tip of the needle and under your thumb.

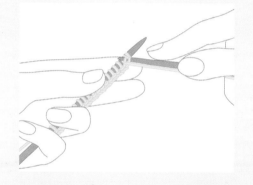

4. Then, hold the yarn and the needle in your right hand, and push the tip of the right-hand needle down until the tip touches the other needle.

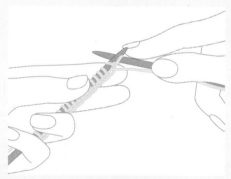

5. Then, slide the tip of the needle behind the left-hand one and push the needle up so that the stitch is a little way away from the tip.

These squares are knitted with different combinations of knit and purl stitches.

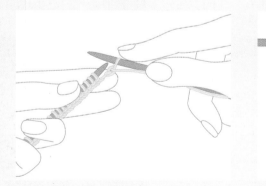

6. Gently slide the stitch on the left-hand needle off the tip of the needle – you now have a purl stitch on the right-hand needle.

7. Continue doing each stitch in the same way until the end of the row. Swap the needle with the stitches to your left hand and purl more rows.

Stocking stitch

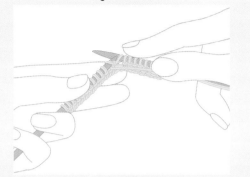

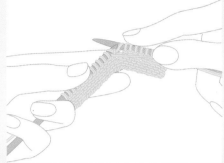

1. To do a square of stocking stitch, cast on 21 stitches, then knit a row in knit stitch. Bring the yarn to the front and do a row in purl stitch.

2. Then, move the yarn to the back of your knitting and do another row in knit stitch. Bring the yarn to the front again and do a purl row.

3. Continue doing alternate rows of knit, then purl stitch. As you knit, your knitting will be smooth on one side and bumpy on the other.

Purl stitch

Stocking stitch

Two rows of knit stitch, one row of purl stitch

Reverse side of stocking stitch

Three rows of knit stitch, three rows of purl stitch

Knit one, purl one

These pages show you how to do rib stitch, which is a combination of knit and purl stitches. It is also sometimes known as ribbing. To practice the ribbed pattern, cast on an even number of stitches.

You can also create different patterns or textures in your knitting by changing the order in which you knit or purl stitches.

Rib stitch

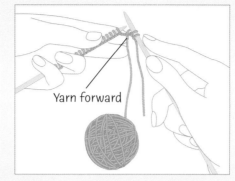

Yarn forward

1. Cast on 24 stitches. Knit the first two stitches in the row in knit stitch. Then, bring the yarn forward between the two needles.

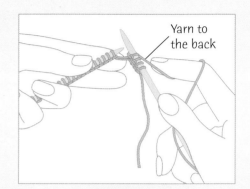

Yarn to the back

2. With the yarn in front, purl the next two stitches in the row. Then, take the yarn to the back, between the two needles again.

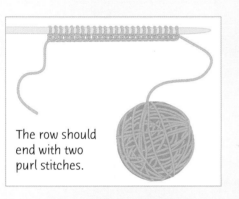

The row should end with two purl stitches.

3. Continue doing two knit stitches with the yarn at the back, followed by two purl stitches with the yarn in front, to the end of the row.

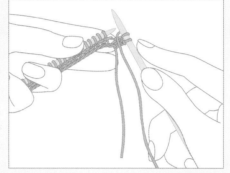

4. Start the next row with two knit stitches again, followed by two purl. Always have the yarn at the back for knit, and at the front for purl stitches.

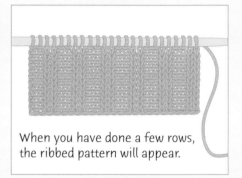

When you have done a few rows, the ribbed pattern will appear.

5. If you lose track of whether you should be knitting or purling, do purl stitches if the next two stitches are bumpy, otherwise do knit stitches.

Moss stitch

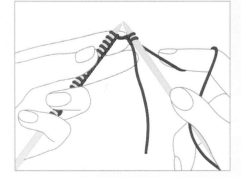

1. Cast on an uneven number of stitches. Knit one stitch, then bring the yarn forward. Purl the next stitch, then take the yarn to the back again.

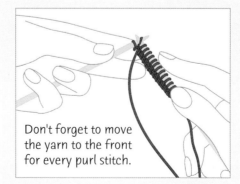

Don't forget to move the yarn to the front for every purl stitch.

2. Continue doing one knit stitch, followed by one purl stitch to the end of the row. The last stitch in the row should be a knit stitch.

This bumpy stitch is called moss stitch.

3. Continue starting each row with a knit stitch. If you're not sure which stitch to do, knit if the stitch on the row below is bumpy, otherwise purl.

Rib stitch

Moss stitch

Basketweave stitch

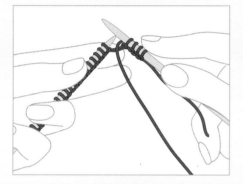

The cushions on pages 26-27 have squares knitted with rib stitch, moss stitch and basketweave stitch.

Basketweave stitch

1. Cast on 24 stitches. Knit the first four stitches in the row with knit stitch. Then, bring the yarn to the front and purl the next four stitches.

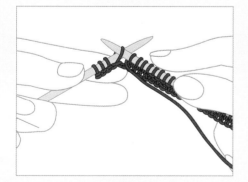

2. Continue along the row doing four knit stitches, then four purl stitches and so on. The last four stitches in the row should be purl stitches.

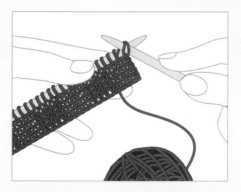

3. Repeat four knit, then four purl stitches for three more rows. Then, start the next row (row 5) with four purl followed by four knit stitches.

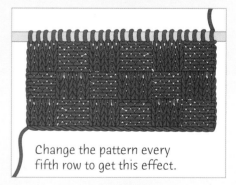

Change the pattern every fifth row to get this effect.

4. Continue knitting like this until you have completed four more rows. Then, swap back to starting the row with four knit stitches again.

Cell phone cover

This little cover is made from a strip of stocking stitch knitting (one row knit, one row purl). They are ideal for cell phones or mp3 players. The pattern shown here is for a small phone or mp3 player, but if you want to make a larger one, cast on 20 stitches and make your knitting 11 inches long.

You will need:
1 x 1¾ ounce ball light weight yarn
a pair of 4.5mm (US 7) knitting needles
a sewing needle with a large eye

Unwind 16 inches of yarn and make a slip knot.
Cast on 16 stitches.
First row - knit (K) to end.
Next row - purl (P) stitch.
Repeat the last two rows until your knitting measures 10 inches.
Cast off the stitches following the instructions on page 12.
Follow the instructions below for sewing it together.

Joining up

Push in a pin to secure it.

1. With the bumpy side of your knitting facing you, fold up the bottom of your knitting, leaving about 1½ inches at the top.

2. Thread a blunt needle with the yarn left from casting off. Then, pick up a stitch from the edge underneath, and pull the needle through.

3. Stitch the seam together following the instructions for mattress stitch below. Then, join the other side together in the same way.

Mattress stitch

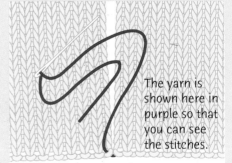

The yarn is shown here in purple so that you can see the stitches.

1. Thread a needle with your yarn and secure it to one edge. Then, pick up a stitch from the opposite edge and pull the yarn through.

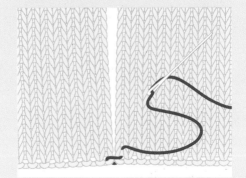

2. Then, pick up the horizontal stitch between the first and second stitches of the opposite edge. Then, pull the yarn through gently.

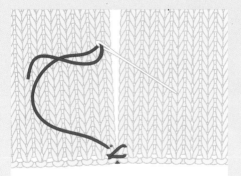

3. Push your needle into the horizontal stitch between the first and second stitches on the other edge, and pull the yarn through again.

The striped phone cover on the left is knitted in rib stitch (see page 18).

Find out on page 56 how to knit arms like the ones on this monster cover. The felt teeth and eyes are glued on.

See pages 38-39 for how to add a button and buttonhole loop to your cover.

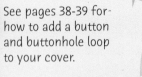

4. Continue picking up stitches from opposite edges. As you stitch, pull the yarn tight every so often so that the seam closes.

Pretty little bags

These little bags would make a lovely present. You could put a little gift inside or fill them with wrapped candies or chocolates.

You will need:
1 x 1¾ ounce ball of medium or light weight yarn
a pair of 4mm (US 6) knitting needles
20 inches of narrow ribbon
a sewing needle with a large eye

Keeping count

Knitters have different ways of keeping count of where they are in a pattern. You could use a pencil to tick off each row on the page as you finish it, or you could keep a tally on a sticky note, making a mark when you finish each row.

Unwind about 20 inches of yarn, then make a slip knot.
Cast on 23 stitches.
First row - knit (K) 1 stitch, purl (P) 1 stitch, repeat these two stitches to the end of the row.
Repeat this row four more times.
Next row - K to end.
Next row - P to end.
Carry on knitting in stocking stitch (K 1 row, P 1 row) until your knitting measures 4¼ inches, ending with a purl row.
Next row - P to end.
Next row - P to end.
Next row - K to end.
Next row - P to end.
Next row - K to end.
Repeat the last 5 rows four more times.
Next row - P to end.
Starting with a K row, carry on knitting in stocking stitch until your knitting measures 11½ inches.
Next row - K1, P1, repeat these stitches to the end of the row.
Repeat this row four more times.
Cast off, then follow the steps for making up the bag.

To knit a plain bag like this green one, do the first 5 rows, then do stocking stitch until your knitting measures 11½ inches, then do the last 5 rows.

Making up the bag

1. Fold your knitting in half. Follow the steps on page 20 to sew the sides of the bag together. Thread the ribbon onto the large needle.

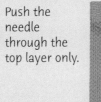

Push the needle through the top layer only.

2. Push the needle into the middle of the bag, about 1¼ inches down. Bring the needle out to the front, two stitches away from where it went in.

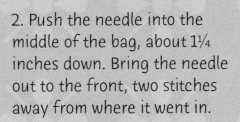

3. Hold the loose end of the ribbon, then gently pull the ribbon through the knitting until the loose end is about 8 inches long.

4. Push the needle back into the knitting, two stitches away from where the ribbon comes out, then bring it out to the front again.

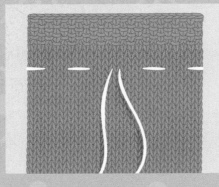

5. Continue weaving the ribbon through the stitches, at the same distance from the top, all the way around to where you started.

6. Gently slip the ribbon out of the needle. Pull the two ends to gather the top of the bag, then tie them in a little bow to secure them.

Handbags

These handbags are perfect for carrying small items such as a purse, keys and a cell phone. The instructions below are for a bag knitted in two colours with a moss stitch border.

You will need:
2 x 1¾ ounce balls of light weight yarn (each ball a different color)
1 pair of 4.5mm (US 7) knitting needles
a sewing needle with a large eye

Unwind a piece of yarn 4 feet long, then make a slip knot.
Cast on 45 stitches.
First row - knit (K) 1 stitch, purl (P) 1 stitch, repeat these two stitches to the end of the row.
Repeat this row until the border measures 1½ inches.
Next row - join on the other ball of yarn and, starting with a K row, do stocking stitch (K 1 row, P 1 row) until your knitting measures 10¼ inches, ending on a P row.
Next row - join on the first ball of yarn again and K to end.
Next row - K1, P1, repeat these two stitches to the end of the row.
Repeat this row until the border measures 1½ inches.
Cast off.

For the handles:
Cast on 12 stitches with the same yarn that you used for the main part of the bag.
First row - K to end.
Next row - P to end.
Continue knitting in stocking stitch (K 1 row, P 1 row) until your knitting measures 8¾ inches.
Cast off, then make another handle.
Follow the steps below for making up the bag.

Making up the bag

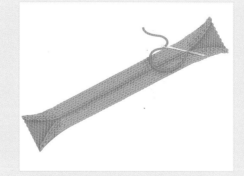

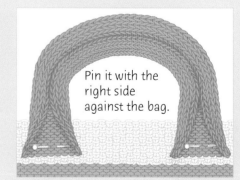

Pin it with the right side against the bag.

1. Thread the needle with yarn. Fold the bag in half, then sew the sides together with mattress stitch (see the steps on page 20).

2. Starting 1¼ inches from one end, sew the sides of each handle together with mattress stitch. Stop stitching about 1¼ inches before the other end.

3. Open out the ends of a handle and pin them inside the top of the bag, like this. Then, cut a piece of yarn and thread it onto the needle.

The tops of these bags aren't secure, so it would be a good idea to sew on a couple of snaps inside.

Find out on page 38 how to knit a bow and sew on a button.

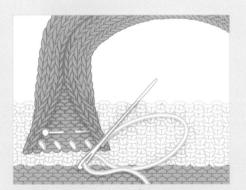

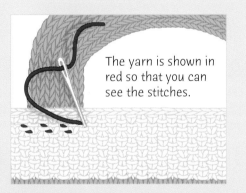

The yarn is shown in red so that you can see the stitches.

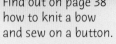

4. Tie a knot in the end of the yarn. Sew the bottom edge of the handle onto the bag. Your sewing shouldn't show on the front of the bag.

5. Push the needle through to the front of the bag and sew the handle on near the top of the bag between the knitted stitches, like this.

6. Sew the other end of the handle onto the bag in the same way. Then, sew the other handle onto the other side of the bag.

Cushion cover

The ends of these cushion covers overlap, so you don't need any fastenings. These instructions are for the turquoise cushion cover which fits a 12 x 12 inch cushion pad.

You will need:
4 x 1¾ ounce balls of medium weight yarn
a pair of 5.5mm (US 9) knitting needles
a sewing needle with a large eye

Unwind 4 feet of yarn, make a slip knot and cast on 54 stitches.
First row - knit (K) to end.
Next row - purl (P) to end.
Next row - K to end.
Next row - P to end.
Next row - P to end.
Next row - K to end.
Next row - P to end.
Next row - K to end.
Repeat these eight rows until your knitting measures 28 inches, then cast off.
Follow the steps for stitching the cushion together.

This cushion was made from little squares that were stitched together, then made into a cover.

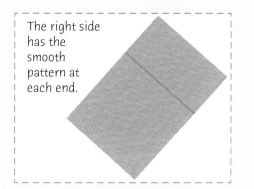

The right side has the smooth pattern at each end.

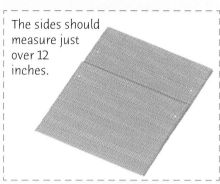

The sides should measure just over 12 inches.

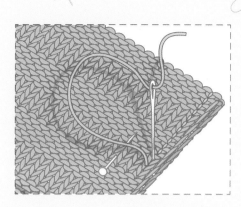

1. Lay your knitting on a flat surface with the right side facing you. Then, fold down the top, so that the folded part measures about 6 inches.

2. Pin the folded part along the edges. Then, fold up the bottom of your knitting so that it overlaps the top part by about 4 inches and pin it.

3. Thread a sewing needle with some yarn and, starting at the top, stitch along the edges with back stitch (see page 58).

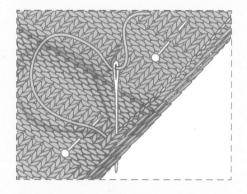

4. When you get to where the folded parts overlap each other, stitch through all the layers. You might need some help with this as it is thick.

Push the cushion through the gap in the middle.

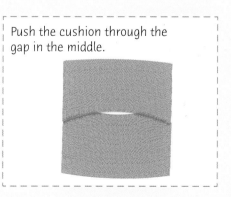

5. Turn the cushion cover inside out. Then, push a cushion into the bottom part. Pull the top part over so that they overlap in the middle.

Ribbed scarf

This scarf has a ribbed texture. It also has a split in it that you can use to secure the ends of the scarf.

You will need:
2 x 1¾ ounce balls of medium weight yarn
1 pair of 5mm (US 8) knitting needles
a stitch holder or very large safety pin

Making the split

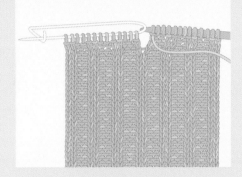

1. *K2, P2* for 12 stitches, then K1 stitch. Then, carefully slip the remaining 13 stitches on the left-hand needle onto a stitch holder.

Unwind 2 feet of yarn, make a slip knot and cast on 26 stitches.
First row - *K2, P2* to the last 2 stitches, K2 (look at page 63 to find out what the *asterisks* mean).
Next row - *P2, K2* to the last 2 stitches, P2.
Repeat these 2 rows until your knitting measures 2½ feet, ending on a *P2, K2* row.

To make the split, follow the instructions in steps 1 and 2.

First row after step 2 - *K2, P2* to the last stitch, K1.
Next row - P1, *K2, P2* to the end of the row.
Repeat the last two rows until the split measures 5 inches, ending on a *K2, P2*, K1 row.
Follow steps 3-5 below.

First row after step 5 - *P2, K2* to the last stitch, P1.
Next row - K1, *P2, K2* to the end of the row.
Repeat the last two rows until this side of the split measures 5 inches, ending with a K1, *P2, K2* row.
Go to steps 6 and 7.

When you have finished step 7 - *K2, P2* to the last 2 stitches, K2.
Next row - *P2, K2* to the last 2 stitches, P2.
Repeat the last two rows until you have knitted 4¾ inches from the end of the split.
Cast off and sew in all the loose ends of yarn.

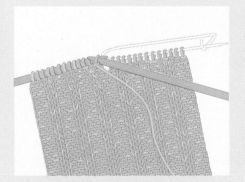

2. Turn your knitting over so that the stitches are on the left-hand needle. P1, *K2, P2* to the end of the row. Then, follow the pattern again.

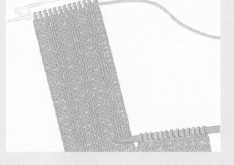

3. Slip the stitches on the stitch holder back onto the empty knitting needle. Then, slip the stitches on the other needle onto the stitch holder.

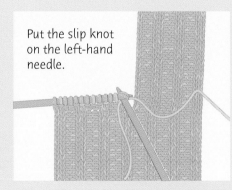

Put the slip knot on the left-hand needle.

4. Cut the yarn from the ball. Tie a slip knot in the yarn and put the slip knot onto the needle. Knit the first stitch and the slip knot together.

Wrap the scarf around your neck, then push one end through the split.

Follow the instructions on pages 30-31 to make pompoms, like these.

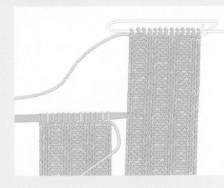

5. Then, *P2, K2* to the end of the row. Continue knitting this thinner piece of the scarf following the main instructions again.

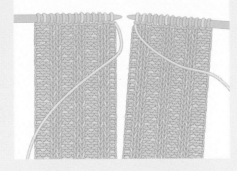

6. On the next row, *P2, K2*, then P the last stitch before the split. Then, slip the stitches on the stitch holder back onto the empty needle.

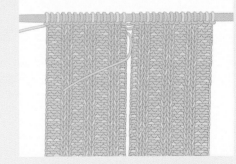

7. Purl the first stitch on the left-hand needle, then continue *K2, P2* to the end of the row. Follow the main instructions again.

Making pompoms

It's easy to make pompoms to decorate things you have knitted. Pompoms are often made using cardboard circles, but these pages show you a much quicker way of making them. Making pompoms is also a very good way of using up left-over yarn. Use any thickness of yarn, except bulky yarn.

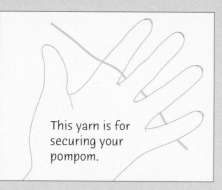

This yarn is for securing your pompom.

1. Cut a piece of yarn about 10 inches long. Then, lay it between your first and middle fingers. Pull it so that the ends are the same length.

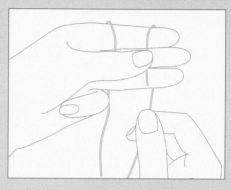

2. Put your three middle fingers together. Then, hold the end of the yarn from the ball with your thumb against your middle finger, like this.

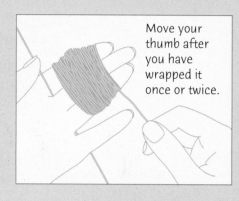

Move your thumb after you have wrapped it once or twice.

3. Wrap the yarn around and around your fingers about 80 times, but be careful not to wrap it so tightly that it hurts your fingers.

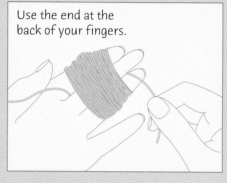

Use the end at the back of your fingers.

4. Hold the end of the yarn which you put between your fingers in step 1. Bring it forward between your middle and third fingers.

5. Then, get someone to tie the loose ends of the yarn around the loops, like this. Don't let them tie the ends too tightly.

You will find that thin yarn makes very fluffy pompoms.

Wrap two colors of yarn around your fingers to make a mottled pompom, like this purple one.

You need to cut quite a lot off the ends.

6. Slip the loops off your fingers carefully. Then, pull the knot as tightly as you can and tie another knot to secure all the loops.

7. Holding the long strands from the knot, cut through the loops. The pompom will be quite scruffy as all the ends are different lengths.

8. Trim the ends to make a neat pompom. Cut off one of the long strands, then use the other one for sewing the pompom onto your knitting.

Simple 'cat' hat

This is a very easy hat to knit. When you put it on, the corners of the hat point up and look like the ears of a cat.

The hat is made from a wide strip of knitting - you have to cast on 100 stitches. The ends of the strip are stitched together at the back, then you simply stitch the hat along the top to complete it.

You only need to know how to do knit stitch to make a hat like this one.

You will need:
1 x 1¾ ounce ball of medium weight yarn
a pair of 4.5 (US 7) knitting needles
a sewing needle with a large eye

Unwind about 10 feet of yarn and make a slip knot.
Cast on 100 stitches.
First row - knit (K) to end.
Then, K every row until your knitting measures 6½ inches from where you cast on.
Cast off.
Follow the step-by-step instructions for making up the hat.

These hats are slightly smaller than actual size.

The bottom of this striped hat is folded up. To make one like this, do 12 rows of knit stitch, then knit 6½ inches in stocking stitch.

Making up the hat

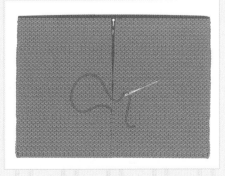

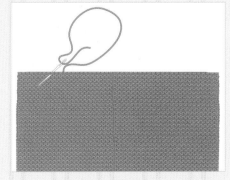

1. Fold your strip of knitting in half and mark the middle point with a pin. Unfold it, then fold in both ends to meet at the pin.

2. Thread the yarn left over from where you cast on, onto a needle with a big eye. Sew the ends together with mattress stitch (see page 20).

3. Thread a new piece of yarn onto the needle. Starting at one end, stitch over and over to join the edges. Then, turn the hat inside out.

Striped bag

When you knit something with narrow stripes, you don't need to cut the yarn every time you change color. Wrap the yarn you're not using around the other one and 'carry' the yarn up the side of your knitting until you need to use it again.

You will need:
2 x 1¾ ounce balls of light weight yarn, each a different color (yarn A and yarn B)
a pair of 4mm (US 6) knitting needles
a sewing needle with a large eye

For the bag, unwind 4 feet of yarn, make a slip knot and cast on 44 stitches from yarn A.
Next row - knit (K) to end.
Next row - purl (P) to end.
Repeat the last 2 rows, twice more (6 rows altogether).
Join on your second color of yarn (yarn B) by tying it around yarn A.
Next row - K to end with yarn B.
Next row - P to end with yarn B.
Repeat the last 2 rows, twice more with yarn B
   (see below how to carry yarn A up the side of your knitting).
Repeat the last 12 rows until the bag measures 23 inches from
   where you cast on, ending with 6 rows of either yarn A or B.
Cast off.

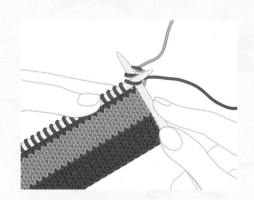

For the strap, cast on 8 stitches from one of the balls of yarn.
Knit every row in knit stitch until the strap measures 4¼ feet.
Cast off.
Follow the instructions opposite for making up the bag.

Carrying the yarn up the side

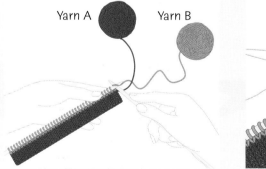

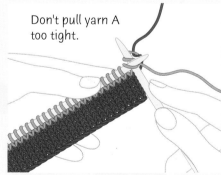

1. When you have finished two rows in yarn B, put your needle into the first stitch in the row and cross yarn A over yarn B.

2. Bring yarn B around the needle to knit the stitch in the normal way. Yarn A will be held by the stitch you have just done.

3. Repeat these steps every two rows, so whichever yarn you are not using is carried up the side of your knitting as you knit the stripes.

The flaps on these two bags have buttons to secure them. Look on page 39 to find out how to sew a buttonhole loop.

These bags are slightly smaller than actual size.

You could knit a matching striped purse (see pages 40-41).

Making up the bag

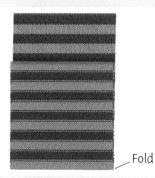

Fold

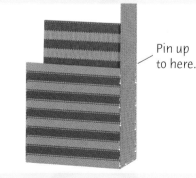

Pin up to here.

1. Lay your knitting with the right side facing you. Fold the bottom end up, as far as the fifth stripe from the top. Mark the fold with a pin.

2. Unfold your knitting and pin one end of the strap to the fold. Then, pin the strap onto your knitting as far as the fifth stripe.

3. Sew the strap on. Then, pin the other end of the strap to the other side of the bag and sew it on in the same way. Turn the bag inside out.

Making fringe

Making fringe with a crochet hook

Making fringe is an easy way to decorate your knitting, especially at the end of a scarf. Both the bunny's scarf on page 13 and simple scarf on page 15 have fringe added to the ends.

These pages show you two different ways of making fringe. The first method uses a crochet hook, but if you don't have one, try the second method.

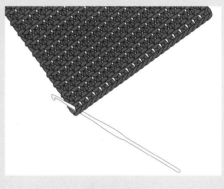

1. Cut two pieces of yarn, just over twice the length that you want your fringe to be. Hold them together and fold them in half.

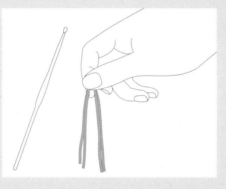

2. Push a crochet hook between the first two stitches on the bottom row. Push it from the back to the front of your knitting.

Don't pull the yarn all the way through the knitting.

3. Loop the pieces of yarn over the crochet hook. Then, gently pull the hook so that the loop goes through to the back of your knitting.

4. Slip the yarn off the crochet hook. Then, put the ends of the yarn through the loop and pull them as tight as you can.

5. Cut more pieces of yarn and add fringe along the edge of your knitting. Finally, trim the ends so that they are the same length.

The fringe on this pink scarf has four strands of thin yarn looped together.

Making fringe without a crochet hook

1. Cut two pieces of yarn, just over twice the length that you want your fringe to be. Hold them together and fold them in half.

2. Twist the fold several times so that the yarn is squeezed together and makes a 'point'. Hold the point between your thumb and first finger.

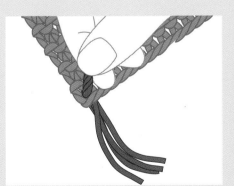

3. Push the point between the first and second stitch of your knitting. Then, use your fingers to pull the folded loop through to the front.

4. Push the loose ends of yarn through the loop, then pull them as tight as you can. Then, add more pieces of yarn (see step 5, opposite).

This scarf has different colors of fringe repeated along its edge.

Buttons and bows

These pages show you how to stitch a button onto your knitting for decoration, or for securing a flap on a bag. There are also steps to show you how to make a loop to go around a button, and how to knit a pretty bow.

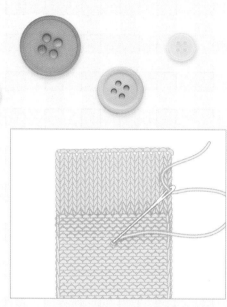

Sewing on a button

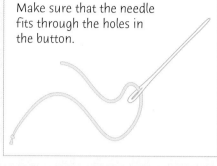

Make sure that the needle fits through the holes in the button.

1. Thread a needle with a large eye with a piece of your knitting yarn. Then, tie a little knot near one end of the yarn.

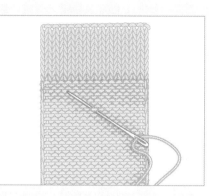

2. Decide where you want to sew on your button. Then, on the back of your knitting, push the needle through a stitch and pull it tight.

3. Push the needle through the same stitch again to secure it. Then, push the needle through onto the right side of your knitting.

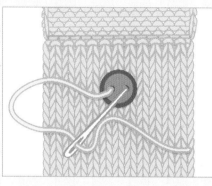

4. Turn your knitting inside out, then push the needle up through one of the holes in the button. Then, stitch down through the other hole.

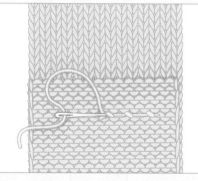

5. Stitch through the button again. Then, on the back of your knitting, weave the yarn through several stitches to secure it (see page 58).

Knitting a bow

You will need:
1 x 1¾ ounce ball of angora yarn
a pair of 4mm (US 6) knitting
    needles

Unwind 12 inches of yarn,
    make a slip knot and cast
    on 10 stitches.
First row - K to end.
Next row - P to end.
Repeat these two rows until
    your knitting measures 16
    inches, then cast off.

Adjust the bow to make it neat before you stitch it together.

Tie the strip of knitting into a bow. Then, do several little stitches on the back of the bow to secure the knot and the ends.

For a striped bow,
swap colors every
two rows.

The flap on this
cell phone cover
is secured with a
button.

A buttonhole loop

Sew the button on
before you start to
make the loop.

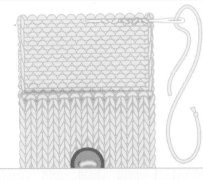

1. To make a buttonhole loop,
like those on the phone
covers on page 21, thread a
piece of yarn onto a needle
and tie a knot in one end.

2. Weave the yarn through
the stitches along the edge of
the flap to secure it. Stop
weaving level with the side of
the button.

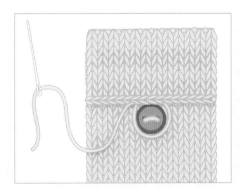

Hold the loop
as you pull
the yarn.

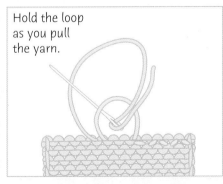

Slide the stitches
around the loop
so that they sit
together tightly.

3. Loop the yarn around the
button and do a small stitch.
Then, slip the loop off the
button. Pull the loop a little
tighter and do another stitch.

4. Put the needle into the loop,
then over the yarn, like this.
Pull gently and a stitch will
form around the loop. Slide it
to the end of the loop.

5. Repeat step 4 again and
again around the loop. When
you come to the other end of
the loop, secure the yarn with
several small stitches.

Little purse

The flaps on these purses are shaped by slipping stitches over each other and knitting other stitches together.

You will need:
2 x 1¾ ounce balls of light weight yarn (each ball a different color)
1 pair of 4mm (US 6) knitting needles
a sewing needle with a large eye

Unwind about 20 inches from one of your yarns (yarn A) and make a slip knot.
Cast on 25 stitches.
First row - knit (K) to end.
Next row - purl (P) to end.
Attach yarn B by tying it around yarn A (keep yarn A attached).
Next row - K to end with yarn B.
Next row - P to end with yarn B.
Next row - repeat the last two rows with yarn A (taking it up the edge of the last two rows - see page 34).
Continue doing stocking stitch (K 1 row, P 1 row), swapping the color every two rows. Continue until your knitting measures 8 inches, ending on a P row with yarn A.
Next row - K1, slip 1, K1, pass the slipped stitch over (see page 55), knit to the last 3 stitches, K2 together, K1.
Next row - P to end.
Repeat the last two rows until 5 stitches remain.
Next row - P to end.
Cast off.

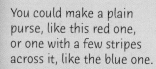

You could make a plain purse, like this red one, or one with a few stripes across it, like the blue one.

40

Find out on page 59
how to sew these daisies.

Making up the purse

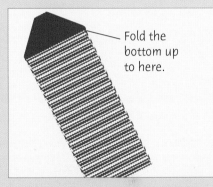

Fold the bottom up to here.

1. Lay your knitting with the wrong side (the bumpy side) facing up. Then, fold the bottom of the knitting up as far as the flap.

You can buy large snaps, like the one on this purse, from the sewing section in a department store.

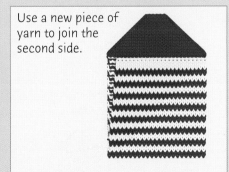

Use a new piece of yarn to join the second side.

2. Thread the yarn left from your cast on, onto a needle and sew up the side using mattress stitch (see page 20). Join up the other side, too.

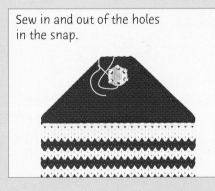

Sew in and out of the holes in the snap.

3. If you want to add a snap to secure the flap, separate a snap. Use ordinary sewing thread to sew one piece onto the flap.

Position the snap so that the flap closes flat.

4. Fold the flap over and position the other half of the snap on the purse. Sew it on. Then, stitch a button on top of the flap (see page 38).

Beanie hat

This beanie hat isn't hard to knit, but you do need to keep a careful count of the rows. Mark them as you knit them (see page 22), so that when you pick up your knitting again you know which row to knit next.

You will need:
2 x 1¾ ounce balls of medium weight yarn
a pair of 4.5mm (US 7) knitting needles
a sewing needle with a large eye

Unwind about 5 feet of yarn and make a slip knot.
Cast on 84 stitches.
First row - knit (K) to end.
Next row - purl (P) to end.
Continue knitting in stocking stitch (K 1 row, P 1 row) until your
   knitting measures 6½ inches, ending with a P row.
Next row - *K6, K2 together (tog)* repeat to the last 4 stitches,
   K4 (74 stitches remaining).
Next row - *P6, P2 tog* repeat to the last 2 stitches, P2
   (65 sts remaining).
Next row - *K5, K2 tog* repeat to the last 2 stitches, K2
   (56 sts remaining).
Next row - *P5, P2 tog* repeat to the last 7 stitches, P3, P2 tog,
   P2 (48 sts remaining).
Next row - *K4, K2 tog* repeat to the end of the row
   (40 sts remaining).
Next row - *P4, K2 tog* repeat to the last 4 stitches, P4
   (34 sts remaining).
Next row - *K3, K2 tog* repeat to the last 4 stitches, K4
   (28 sts remaining).
Next row - *P3, P2 tog* repeat to the last 3 stitches, P3
   (23 sts remaining).
Next row - *K2, K2 tog* repeat to the last 3 stitches, K3
   (18 sts remaining).
Next row - *P2, P2 tog* repeat to the last 2 stitches, P2
   (14 sts remaining).
Next row - *K1, K2 tog* repeat to the last 2 stitches, K2
   (10 sts remaining).
Next row - *P2, P2 tog* repeat to the last stitch, P2
   (8 sts remaining).
Next row - *K2 tog* repeat 3 times (4 sts remaining).
Follow the step-by-step instructions for making up the hat.

Making up the hat

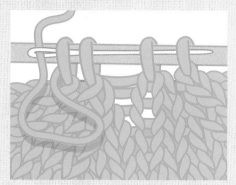

1. Cut the yarn, leaving a 10 inches 'tail,' then thread the tail onto a needle. Push the needle through the four remaining stitches.

2. Slip the stitches off the knitting needle, then pull the yarn tight. Sew one or two little stitches to secure the knitted stitches.

3. With the right side facing you, pin the sides of the hat together. Then, join them neatly with mattress stitch (see page 20).

The bottom of the beanie hat will roll up naturally on its own.

These hats were decorated with knitted flowers and leaves from pages 52-55.

43

Little heart cushion

These little cushions are shaped by increasing and decreasing the number of stitches you are knitting.

For one cushion, you will need:
1 x 1¾ ounce ball of angora yarn
a pair of 5mm (US 8) knitting needles
a sewing needle with a large eye and some stuffing fiber

Unwind 8 inches of yarn, make a slip knot and cast on 4 stitches.
Do 2 rows of stocking stitch (K 1 row, P 1 row).
Next row - increase (inc) 1 stitch in every stitch - see right (8 sts).
Next row - P to end.
Next row - cast on 2 stitches at the beginning of the next 2 rows - see page 62 (12 sts).
Inc 1 stitch at the beginning and end of the next 9 rows (30 sts).
Next row - P to end.
Next row - Inc 1 stitch at the beginning and end of the next row.
Next row - P to end.
Repeat the last 2 rows 4 more times (40 sts).
Then, do 10 rows of stocking stitch.
Next row - slip 1 stitch onto the right-hand needle, K1, pass the slipped stitch over the knitted stitch (psso), K to the last 2 stitches, K2 tog (38sts).
Next row - P to end.
Repeat the last two rows (36 sts).
Next row - slip 1, K1, psso, K14 stitches, K2 tog.
Put the 18 stitches on the left-hand needle onto a stitch holder.
Turn your knitting around, then P2 tog, P12, P2 tog (14 sts).
Next 3 rows - do in stocking stitch - K2 tog on a K row or P2 tog on a P row, at the beginning and ends of the rows (8 sts).
Next row - P to end.
Cast off and cut the yarn.
Put the stitches on the stitch holder onto a knitting needle.
Make a slip knot, then slip it, and the first stitch, onto the right-hand needle. Then, K1, pass the slipknot and the slip stitch over the knitted stitch, K to the last 2 stitches, K2 tog (16 sts).
Next row - P2 stitches tog, P to the last 2 stitches, P2 tog.
Next 3 rows - do in stocking stitch - K2 tog on a K row or P2 tog on a P row, at the beginning and ends of the rows (8 sts).
Next row - P to end.
Cast off and make another heart, then follow the steps for making up the cushion.

Increasing a stitch

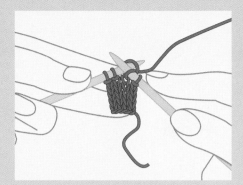

1. To increase a stitch on a knit row, do a knit stitch as normal, but don't slide the stitch off the left-hand needle yet.

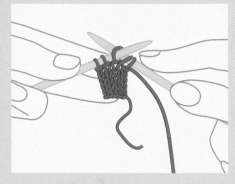

2. Then, take the tip of the right-hand needle around to the back of the left-hand one and push it through the back of the same stitch.

Take the yarn around the needles like this.

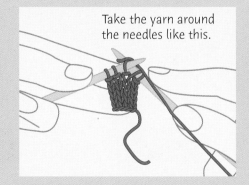

3. Take the yarn around the tip of the right-hand needle and knit the stitch, sliding it off onto the needle as usual. You now have an extra stitch.

One side of your cushion will be smooth and the other side will have a bumpy texture.

Making up the cushion

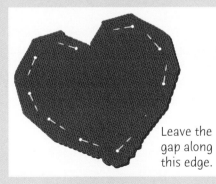

Leave the gap along this edge.

1. Lay one heart on top of the other, both with the smooth side facing up. Then, pin them around the edge, leaving a gap at one side.

2. Use back stitch to join the two hearts together (see page 58), but leave the gap so that you can stuff the cushion.

3. Turn the cushion inside out, then fill it with stuffing. Pin the open edge together and stitch over and over the edges to join the gap.

Felted bag

If a sweater made from 100% wool is washed in hot water, the wool shrinks and mats together to make a thick felty material. You can do this intentionally to your knitting to make a sturdy bag.

You will need:
6 x 3½ ounce balls of 100% bulky or super bulky weight wool yarn (avoid anything that says 'machine washable' on the label as it won't felt)
a pair of 12mm (US 17) knitting needles

Unwind 6½ feet of yarn and make a slip knot.
Cast on 30 stitches.
First row - knit (K) to end.
Next row - purl (P) to end.
Repeat these two rows until your knitting measures 2½ feet.
Cast off.

For the handles (knit 2):
Cast on 4 stitches.
First row - K to end.
Next row - P to end.
Repeat these two rows until your knitting measures 2½ feet.
Cast off.

This is what the knitting looked like before it was felted.

Making up and felting the bag

You may find it easier to sew if you use thinner yarn.

1. Fold the bag in half and pin the sides. Thread a needle with some yarn, then join the sides using mattress stitch (see page 20).

2. Turn the bag inside out and pin one handle to each side. Sew the ends of the handles around their sides and along the top edge of the bag.

The towel will help to move the bag around in the water.

3. Put the finished bag into a washing machine along with a large old towel. Add some laundry detergent.

4. Set the washing machine for a half load at a 60° (140°F) temperature. Then, turn it on and let it run through its washing and rinsing cycles.

The thick felted fabric may take a while to dry.

5. Take your bag out of the washing machine. The stitches will have felted together. Lay your bag on a flat surface and let it dry.

Find out on pages 52-55 how to make the flower and leaves.

47

Felted Flowers

The flowers on these pages are made from pieces of knitting that were then felted in a washing machine. This is a good way of using up left-over yarn but make sure the yarn is 100% wool. However, some 100% wool yarns say 'machine washable' on the ball band - don't use these as the yarn won't felt.

To start, unwind about 2 feet of yarn, make a slip knot, then cast on 40 stitches.

You will need:
100% wool medium or light weight yarn
a pair of 4.5mm (US 7) or 5mm (US 8)
   knitting needles
a sewing needle and thread

Do two pieces of knitting so that the middle of the flower will be a different color.

1. Knit in stocking stitch (K 1 row, P 1 row) until your knitting measures 8 inches. Then, cast off. Knit a second piece in another color.

2. Felt the two pieces of knitting in a washing machine, following steps 3 to 5 on pages 46-47. Leave them to dry completely.

3. Draw a simple flower on a piece of paper and cut it out. Pin it onto one of the pieces of felted knitting and cut around it.

4. Cut a circle from the other piece of knitting and pin it in the middle of the flower. Sew little stitches over the edges of the circle to secure it.

You could cut a leaf shape and sew it onto the back of a flower.

The middle of this pale blue flower was decorated with beads before it was stitched onto the flower.

48

You could sew a safety pin onto the back of a flower and pin it onto your clothes.

This large pink flower had individual petals sewn onto the back of a circle.

To make petals like the ones above, felt a piece of striped knitting.

49

Shoulder wrap

This shoulder wrap is reversible if you choose not to make the knitted flower.

You will need:
3 x 1¾ ounce balls of light weight yarn
a pair of 4.5mm (US 7) knitting needles
a sewing needle with a large eye

Unwind a piece of yarn about 4 feet long and make a slip knot.
Cast on 45 stitches.
First row - * knit (K) 1, purl (P) 1* repeat until the end of the row.
Next row - K to end.
Repeat these two rows until your knitting measures 3½ feet.
Cast off, then follow the instructions below for making up the wrap.

Making up the wrap

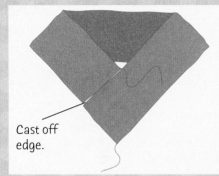

Cast off edge.

1. Fold your knitting around so that the end where you have cast off meets the side of the other end of the wrap, like this.

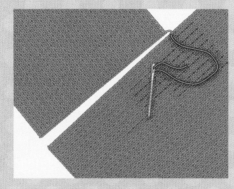

2. Thread the yarn left from where you cast off onto a needle. Pick up a stitch from the other edge of the wrap and pull the yarn tight.

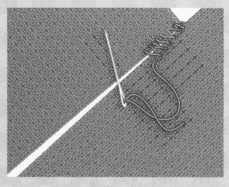

3. Then, pick up a stitch from the first edge again and pull the yarn tight. Continue stitching through alternate edges to join the seam.

Flower decoration

4. To secure the end of the yarn, sew through the last stitch again, then weave the yarn in and out of the stitches in the seam.

1. To make the petals of the flower, follow the pattern for the leaves on page 54. You will need to knit six petals altogether.

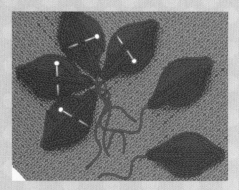

2. Sew in the ends of the yarn where you cast off, but leave the loose cast-on ends. Lay the petals in a flower shape, then pin them onto the wrap.

If you add a flower decoration to your wrap, it won't be reversible, as you'll see the stitches where you've attached the petals.

This wrap is smaller than actual size. It will fit around your shoulders.

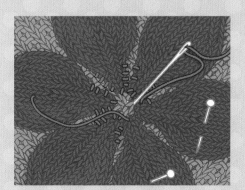

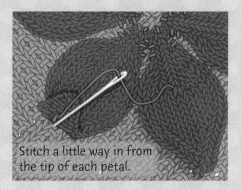
Stitch a little way in from the tip of each petal.

3. Thread a loose cast-on end onto a needle, then do little stitches around the end of a petal to secure it. Sew on the other petals in the same way.

4. Then, thread another piece of yarn onto a needle. Do one or two stitches to secure the other ends of the petals to the wrap.

5. For the middle of the flower, place a big button over the ends of the petals. Sew it on using yarn or ordinary sewing thread.

Knitted flowers

These flowers use a stitch, called yarn over, that makes a hole in your knitting and gives it a lacy effect. You can use these flowers to decorate a bag (see page 46) or a hat (see page 43), or stitch a safety pin to the back and wear them on your clothes.

For a flower, you will need:
1 x 1¾ ounce ball of medium or light weight yarn
a pair of 5mm (US 8) knitting needles
a sewing needle with a large eye

Unwind 8 inches of yarn, make a slip knot, then cast on 4 stitches.

Next 3 rows - knit (K) to end.

Next row - K1, then take the yarn over (YO) before the next stitch (see the opposite page), repeat *K1, YO* to the end of the row, ending with K1 (7 stitches).

Next 2 rows - K to end.

Next row - *K1, YO* to the end of the row, ending with K1 (13 stitches).

Next 2 rows - K to end.

Next row - *K1, YO* to the end of the row, ending with K1 (25 stitches).

Next 2 rows - K to end.

Next row - *K1, YO* to the end of the row, ending with K1 (49 stitches). The stitches will be bunched tightly together.

Next 2 rows - K to end.

Cast off loosely.

Find out on pages 54-55 how to knit a leaf to add to your flowers.

Yarn over (YO)

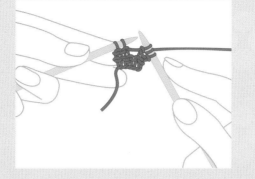

1. Knit one stitch, then bring the yarn from the ball forward between the two needles, as if you are going to do a purl stitch.

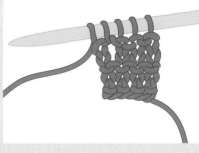

2. Then, knit the next stitch as usual, taking the yarn over the right-hand needle and around the tip. This creates an extra stitch.

3. When you knit the next row, knit the extra stitch in the normal way. This creates a hole between the stitches in the row below.

Sewing the flower

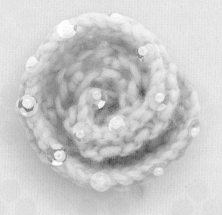

You can sew sequins and beads along the edge of a flower to make it sparkly.

1. Before you sew your flower together, pull the stitches between your fingers all the way along the cast off edge, to make it really loose.

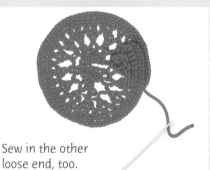

Sew in the other loose end, too.

2. Twist the flower into a spiral. Thread a needle onto the loose yarn in the middle and secure the spiral with little stitches on the back.

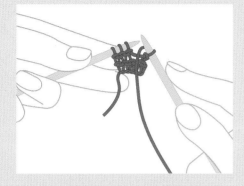

Knitted leaves

These knitted leaves can be used to decorate knitted flowers (see pages 52-53), or you can use them as petals to make large flowers to stitch onto your knitting (see page 51).

You will need:
1 x 1¾ ounce ball of medium or light weight yarn
a pair of 5mm (US 8) knitting needles

Unwind about 8 inches of yarn, make a slip knot, then cast on 3 stitches.
Do 4 rows of stocking stitch (K 1 row, P 1 row), starting with a knit row.
Next row - K1, make 1 stitch (see below how to do this), K1, make 1, K1 (5 stitches).
Next row - P to end.
Next row - K2, make 1, K1, make 1, K2 (7 stitches).
Next row - P to end.
Next row - K3, make 1, K1, make 1, K3 (9 stitches).
Next row - P to end.
Next row - K4, make 1, K1, make 1, K4 (11 stitches).
Next row - P to end.
Do four rows of stocking stitch, starting with a knit row.
Next row - K1, slip one stitch, K1, pass the slip stitch over the knitted stitch (see the opposite page), K to the last three stitches, K2 together, K1.
Next row - P to end.
Repeat the last two rows twice more until you have 5 stitches left on your needle, ending with a purl row.
Next row - K1, slip 1, pass the slip stitch over. Then, slip the last stitch on the right-hand needle back onto the left-hand needle, K2 together, K1.
Cut the yarn and thread it onto a needle. Thread the yarn through the stitches, then secure the yarn with little stitches.

Making a stitch

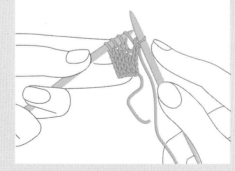
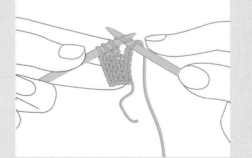

You could felt these leaves (see page 46).

1. Put the left-hand needle under the loop between the stitch you have just knitted and the one you're about to knit, from front to back.

2. Put the right-hand needle into the back of the loop and knit the stitch in the way that you would normally do a knit stitch. You have an extra stitch.

This red flower has five 'petals' sewn together. The leaf was then stitched on at the back.

Slipping a stitch and passing it over

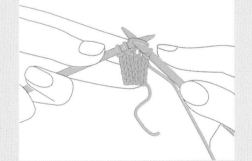

1. Slip the right-hand needle into the next stitch on the left-hand needle, then slip the stitch onto the right-hand needle without knitting it.

2. Knit the next stitch as usual. Then, use the left-hand needle to lift the slipped stitch over the stitch you have just knitted.

Little monster toys

These little toys don't take very long to knit and are a great way of using up yarn you have left over from other knitting projects.

You will need:
1 x 1¾ ounce ball of medium weight yarn
a pair of 4.5mm (US 7) knitting needles
stuffing fiber or cotton

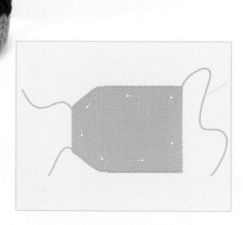

This monster's eyes were cut from felt and glued on.

For the body (make 2):
First row - unwind about 20 inches of yarn, make a slip knot and cast on 20 stitches.
Next row - knit (K) to end.
Next row - purl (P) to end.
Repeat the last two rows until your knitting measures 3 inches.
Next row - K2, slip the first stitch over the second one then K to the last 2 stitches, K2 together.
Next row - P to end.
Repeat the last two rows until you have 12 stitches left.
Next row - P to end, then cast off.

For the arms (make 2):
Cast on 5 stitches.
First row - K to end.
Next row - P to end.
Repeat these two rows until your knitting measures 2¾ inches.
Cast off.

For the legs (make 2):
Cast on 7 stitches.
First row - K to end.
Next row - P to end.
Repeat these two rows until your knitting measures 4 inches.
Cast off.

Follow the step-by-step instructions for making up the monster.

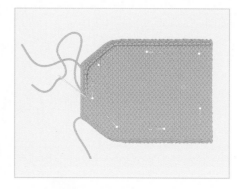

Push the stuffing inside as you stitch.

1. Pin the two parts of the body with the right sides together. Thread the yarn left from casting on, onto a sewing needle.

2. Sew all the way around the sides using little back stitches (see page 58). Leave the bottom edge open so that you have a gap for stuffing.

3. Turn the body inside out and stuff it with stuffing fiber or cotton. Then, sew over and over along the bottom edge to close it.

These monsters mouths were cut from felt or stitched on with embroidery thread.

This little monster's yellow ears are leaves from pages 54-55.

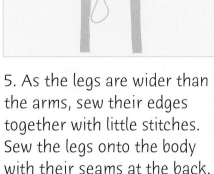

4. The edges of the arms will have rolled in, so they don't need to be stitched. Use little stitches to attach an arm to each side of the body.

5. As the legs are wider than the arms, sew their edges together with little stitches. Sew the legs onto the body with their seams at the back.

6. Use ordinary sewing thread or embroidery thread to sew on two little beads or buttons for eyes (see page 38 for how to sew on a button).

Sewing stitches

Sewing with embroidery thread or yarn is a good way to decorate your knitting. These pages show you how to sew simple stitches. Back stitch can also be used to join two pieces of knitting together (see the heart cushions on page 45).

Before you sew any of the stitches, thread a needle and tie a knot at one end.

Securing the thread

Before you begin sewing, run your threaded needle through several stitches on the back of your knitting. This will secure the knot.

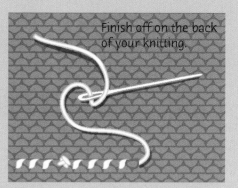

Finish off on the back of your knitting.

When you have finished, sew through a stitch, then through the same stitch again. Run the needle through a few more stitches, then cut the thread.

Cross stitch

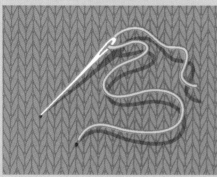

1. Bring the needle up from the back of your knitting and pull the thread through. Push the needle back into the knitting at a diagonal.

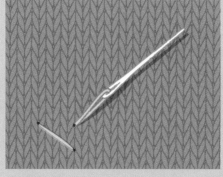

2. Pull the needle down gently to make the stitch. Then, bring the needle back up again, beside the first stitch, like this.

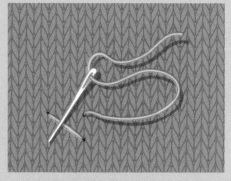

3. Push the needle into your knitting again, so that you make an 'X', like this. Then, pull the needle down to complete the stitch.

Back stitch

1. Bring the needle up from the back and pull the thread through. Then, push the needle back into the knitting a little way away.

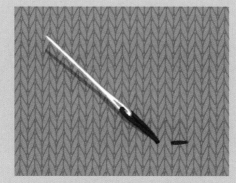

2. Gently pull the thread through. Then, bring the needle up again a little way away from the left-hand end of the first stitch.

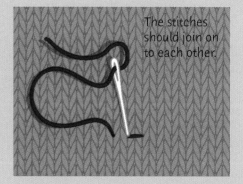

The stitches should join on to each other.

3. Put the needle back into the knitting at the end of the first stitch and pull the thread through. Then, repeat steps 1 and 2 again and again.

Lazy daisy stitch

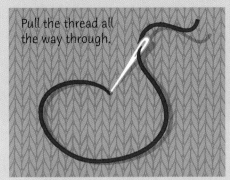
Pull the thread all the way through.

1. Bring the needle up from the back of your knitting where you want a 'petal' to start. Then, push it back into the knitting at the same place.

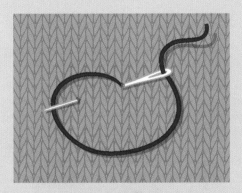

2. Push the tip of the needle up through the knitting again, a little way away, like this, then loop the thread under the tip of the needle.

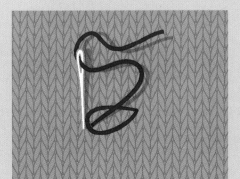

3. Pull the thread gently to make a loop. Then, do a little stitch over the end of the loop and pull your needle back down through your knitting.

Sew five or six 'petals' to make up the flower.

4. To complete the flower, do more stitches in the same way, bringing the thread up near the first stitch each time. Try to keep the stitches even.

This sample shows lots of different ways of decorating your knitting.

Sew some buttons, beads and sequins between your stitches.

For a two-colored line, like the silver and pink one, do a row of stitches, then weave another color in and out of them.

You could sew sequins and beads into the middle of a lazy daisy flower.

Continental knitting

Knit stitch

There are two main ways of doing knit and purl stitches - the 'English' methods, which are explained on pages 10 and 16, and the 'Continental' methods, shown here. The difference is that you hold the yarn from the ball in your left hand, so left-handed people sometimes find this method easier. Cast on about 12 stitches before you begin following these steps.

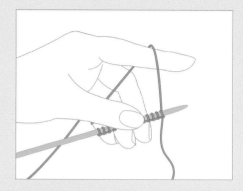
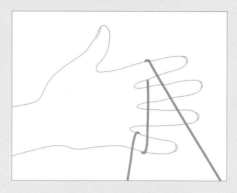

1. Wrap the little finger of your left hand around the yarn once. Then, wrap the yarn over the top of your first finger, like this.

2. Hold the needle with the stitches between the thumb and middle finger of your left hand. Hold your first finger out straight.

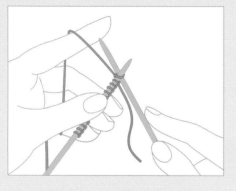
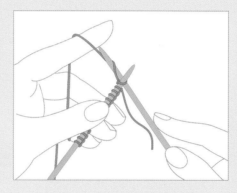
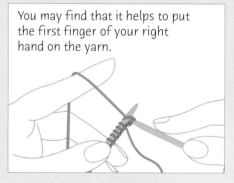

3. Push the tip of the right-hand needle into the first stitch, from the front to the back. The tips of the two needles will be crossed.

4. Then, move the tip of the right-hand needle over the yarn, then under it so that the yarn wraps around the tip of the needle.

You may find that it helps to put the first finger of your right hand on the yarn.

5. Slide the tip of the right-hand needle gently around the left-hand needle, so that you pull a loop of yarn through the stitch.

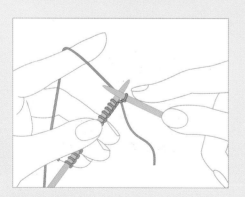
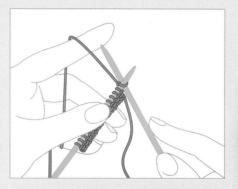

6. Slide the stitch up to the tip of the left-hand needle and off the end of it. You've now knitted one stitch. Keep on knitting along the row.

7. When you've knitted the first row, swap the needles so that the one with the stitches is in your left hand, then knit the stitches again.

Purl stitch

1. Wrap the yarn around your fingers as you did for a knit stitch. Then, bring the yarn from your first finger around to the front of your needles.

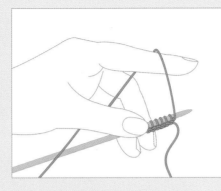

2. Push the tip of the right-hand needle into the first stitch, from the back to the front, so that it crosses over the left-hand one.

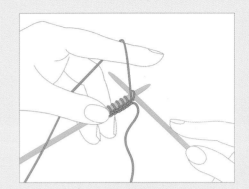

3. Wrap the yarn from your left-hand finger between the two needles. Then, wrap it once around the tip of the right-hand needle, like this.

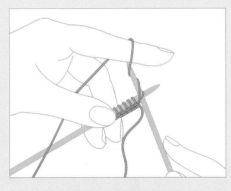

4. Hold the wrapped yarn secure with your thumb. Then, slide the tip of the right-hand needle around the left-hand needle.

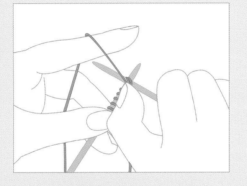

5. Then, slide the tip of the right-hand needle behind the left-hand one and push up so that the new stitch is a little way away from the tip.

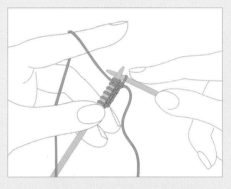

6. Gently slide the stitch on the left-hand needle off the tip of the needle. You now have a new purl stitch on the right-hand needle.

'Continental' knitting looks the same as 'English' knitting.

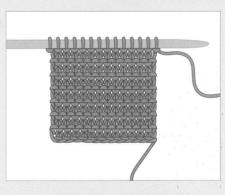

7. Continue knitting purl stitches in this way until the end of the row. Then, swap the needles over and keep on knitting.

More stitches

This page shows you how to cast on extra knit stitches at the beginning of a row, and how to increase a stitch at the end of a row. These stitches increase the number of stitches you have on your needle and help to shape your knitting.

You need to know how to do these stitches for the heart cushion on pages 44-45.

Casting on extra stitches

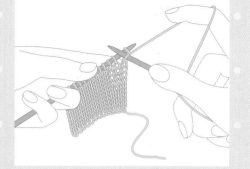

1. Push the right-hand needle into the first stitch in the row and do a knit stitch, but don't slide the loop off the left-hand needle.

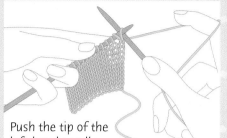

Push the tip of the left-hand needle up into the stitch.

2. Twist the left-hand needle in front of the right-hand one, then push the tip of it under the stitch on the right-hand needle.

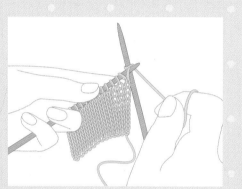

3. Slide the right-hand needle out of the left-hand stitch. You now have an extra stitch. Knit into the new stitch in the usual way and finish the row.

When you increase stitches, it leaves a ragged edge, but this is hidden when you sew your knitting together.

For the heart cushion on pages 44-45, you need to cast on two extra stitches, so follow these steps again to make another new stitch.

Increasing at the end of a row

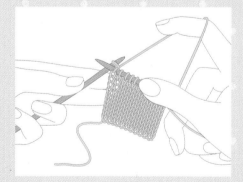

To increase at the end of the row, knit to the last stitch then knit into the front, then the back of the stitch, following the steps on page 44.

Knitting information

Needle size conversions

Here is a conversion chart for the metric, old UK and US knitting needle sizes, used in this book.

Metric	Old UK	US
4mm	8	6
4.5mm	7	7
5mm	6	8
5.5mm	5	9
12mm	-	17

Names of yarns

Different names are given to the different weights or thicknesses of yarn used in this book. Look on pages 6-7 for more about the thickness of different yarns.

4-ply - baby, sport, fine
double knitting - double knit, light worsted, light
aran - worsted, fisherman, medium
chunky - bulky
super chunky - super bulky

Abbreviations

Knitting patterns often use abbreviations for stitches rather than writing everything out in words. Here are the abbreviations used in this book and some common ones which you may find in other knitting patterns.

beg = beginning
CO = cast on
dec = decrease
inc = increase
K = knit stitch
K 2 tog = knit 2 stitches together
LH = left-hand needle
M1 = make one stitch
P = purl stitch
psso = pass slip stitch over

RH = right-hand needle
RS = right side
sl = slip
st st = stocking stitch
sts = stitches
tog = together
WS = wrong side
YB or ytb = yarn to back
YF or ytf = yarn to front
YO = yarn over

Asterisks*

Some of the patterns in this book use an asterisk (*) to mark a set of instructions which need to be repeated, rather than writing the instructions over and over again. For example, '*P2, P2 together*, repeat until the last 2 stitches, P2'. This means that you repeat the stitches inside the asterisks again and again, then purl the last two stitches in the row.

Yarn used for the projects

Here is a list of the yarns that were used for the projects in this book.
p11 - lilac scarf, p12-13 - bunny's scarves and p34-35 - bags, Rowan Handknit DK cotton; p15 - pink scarf, Debbie Bliss Cashmerino chunky; p21 - phone covers, Rowan All Seasons cotton and Rowan Handknit DK cotton; p22-23 - little bags, Debbie Bliss Cathay; p25 - bags, Rowan Calmer; p26-27 - cushions, Rowan Cotton rope and Rowan All Seasons cotton; p29 - scarf, Rowan Summer tweed; p30-31 - pompoms, various double knitting 'superwash' yarns; p32-33 - hats, Debbie Bliss Merino DK; p38-39 - bows, Rowan Kid Classic and Adriafil Carezza angora; p40-41 - purses, Rowan Handknit DK cotton and Rowan Denim; p43 - hats, RYC Cashsoft aran; p45 - cushions, Adriafil Carezza angora; p47 - bag, Rowan Biggy print, p48-49 - flowers, a mixture of 100% wool yarns; p51 - wrap, Rowan Calmer; p52-53 - flowers, Rowan Calmer and Rowan Soft Baby; p54-55 - leaves, Bergère de France Ideal; p56-57 - toys, Adriafil Carezza angora and Bergère de France Ideal.

Index

With thanks to

Kate Buchanan for the patterns on pages 22-23, 24-25, 26-27, 32-33, 34-35, 40-41, 44-45, 46-47, 50-51, 52-53 and 54-55
All the knitters; Hannah Ahmed, Jackie Ellis, Gill Figg, Lynda Harrison, Kitty Evans, Nelupa Hussain, Louise Mitchell,
Vera Pirri and Hanri van Wyk.
Abigail Brown for the bunny on pages 2-3 and 12-13 • Photographic manipulation by John Russell